SWEDISH DEATH CLEANING

A PRACTICAL APPROACH TO DECLUTTER

AND

ORGANIZE YOUR LIFE WHILE PUTTING

YOUR AFFAIRS IN ORDER

By

Emily Jenkins

ISBN-13: 978-1727323221

ISBN-10: 172732322X

INTRODUCTION

A lot of people get chills running through their veins when they hear the word 'death'. Some families do not talk about it at all. For most Americans, the first time talk about death is when they face the loss of a loved one. People generally shy away from the topic of dying. Goose bumps or not, it is a state that we all will come to. The only difference is when and how it will happen.

Proactive Swedes are coming to terms with this fact and are evolving cultural practices that make the idea of death comfortable both for the individual and for the family. One of these practices is death cleaning. Contrary to what its name implies, it is not something that they practice after a death but rather something that takes place before death occurs and for varying lengths of time according to individual preferences. It is a cultural practice that we all can benefit from, dying or not.

In fact, it has more usefulness in helping us organize our lives than we can actually acknowledge. Death cleaning helps us to tidy up our lives and is not as sombre as it sounds.

It is a home organization trend that is getting increasingly popular in western societies and especially in the interior design industry. The death cleaning revolution is sweeping across the United States of America, Sweden, Europe and other western societies because of the mass consumerism and clutter that has not only become associated with the 21st century but has also become an increasing source of worry in these societies. It has gotten everyone talking. The idea was propelled into recognition by a Swedish artist, Margareta Magnusson and has its roots in her book titled The Gentle Art of Swedish Death Cleaning: How to Free Yourself and Your Family From a Lifetime of Clutter.

The actual practice of death cleaning will show you that it is more joyful than it sounds. But before then, as you gct familiar with the death cleaning idea, you will realize that it is not something morbid, gloomy or sad. In fact, it holds more benefits for your overall well-being than Magnusson has pointed out. For example, medical experts are of the opinion that death cleaning can reduce stress. We all know that when an elderly person's house is a mass of clutter, the possibility of tripping and falling is higher.

The only way to avoid such an ugly occurrence is to organize such person's living space so that it is easy to move around. This way, death cleaning can include the smallest details like creating a place to keep your keys so that you do not look for them each time you need them. It can also include getting rid of your staircase by changing your apartment.

The memories that your children and other loved ones you leave behind will have of you can be greatly affected by how organized your later years are. Thus, you can create the memories you want them to have about you by death cleaning.

The Swedes believe that it is your responsibility to make that process of going through your belongings and deciding what to do with them after you are gone less strenuous for your loved ones. This way, you reduce the grief associated with going through a deceased loved one's things and the memories triggered by this. You reduce the pain that your loved ones would feel when they go through your possessions.

You also shorten the process, causing the whole affair to take them lesser periods to accomplish. Consequently, death cleaning is also an act of kindness; something that you will be remembered fondly for.

Stories have been told of the delight that grandchildren experience when their grandparents' material possessions were few and their financial records were well organized making the process of sorting these out easy.

We have also heard of the anguish that heirs feel when they have to face a mountain of possessions. Death cleaning is therefore a proactive way to organize your belongings so that they do not become a burden to your heirs and their families who already have busy lives and may not even want any of it. But this is not all there is to the Scandinavian culture. Death cleaning is like a coin with two sides. It is not all about organizing your affairs to make your estate (in this case, your material possessions) easy to administer. It is also about making your life run with more ease while you are alive. This means that death cleaning is not for the elderly alone. Younger people can also benefit from the practice.

It is a mark of discipline that they can carry throughout life. Their lives become more organized and rid of unnecessary clutter as they go through their possessions often to determine what they truly need and separate them from things that they do not want. It is a way to tidy up their lives. Undoubtedly, such reduced clutter has the potency of making each day easier to go through. Thus, death cleaning is both a way of organizing your home so that it is easy to go through at your death and so that living in it is more enjoyable while you are still alive.

It is a methodical way to make your life simpler and more enjoyable while affording you the opportunity to reflect upon what is truly important and upon the joys in your life.

We have gone into an extensive discussion of the Swedish practice in the subsequent pages and you can be sure that this book offers you a guide through the process in a practical manner.

The book will also show you how to live blissfully after you have gone through the death cleaning process. The crucial process of preparing a will is outlined in the last chapter and you will see that there is no reason for you to keep postponing your death cleaning goals.

CHAPTER ONE

WHAT IS DEATH CLEANING?

The term 'death cleaning' is derived from the Swedish word 'dostadning'. "Do" means death and "standing" means cleaning. Although its translation does not speak of death itself and the dread that comes with it.

Rather, it refers to the art of shedding the unpleasant details of your life instead of leaving them to your bereaved children and other loved ones. It is also about facing death with a prepared posture and with maturity. The art of death cleaning is cleaning out any extraneous possessions that you may have and organizing the rest as you become elderly. It has been defined by Margareta Magnusson as a 'Swedish phenomenon by which the elderly and their families 'set their affairs in order' and Jasmine Hobbs, a cleaning expert at London Cleaning Team thinks that it is 'all about losing everything you don't love or use. And not being afraid to talk about it'.

This goes to show that death cleaning is characterized by being mindful and proactive. As you will see later in this book, it is a methodical and thoughtful approach to decluttering. For the elderly, whatever approach it is they take to death cleaning, it makes the later years comfortable and stress free.

The Swedish decluttering concept reminds us of the inevitability of death and proposes that it is only sensible for us to prepare for it. The proper way to prepare for death's arrival is to pare down and shed our possessions so that they don't become a burden to our heirs and our friends after we have left this earth. So to death clean is to take a look at your belongings one after the other and decide which ones you need. It is a process that induces you to take actions on the things you need and the things you do not need because if you leave them lying around the house and death comes knocking, they might just end up in a dump somewhere even though they were once precious to you.

Death cleaning proposes that you decide what happens to your possessions while you are still alive. You might think that your spouse or children will take care of your things and select which ones they want but they may not want them at all. Also, they may have no time to go through all your things. People lead busy lives today and you will be giving your family an additional burden of trying to find the time to go through your life's possessions.

They may just sigh at the enormous mass of clutter and lock your things away until they can find time to carry out the task. The truth is the time may never come and so what do they do? They will end up giving everything to charity if you are lucky or they would just drive the whole lot to a refuse dump to leave it to fate. If you have lived a fulfilled life, many of these things might be precious to you.

Despite that, you cannot control how your loved ones feel about them. To avoid these kind of occurrences, you need to death clean. You might be saying that you would be dead by then anyway and not care about whatever happens but death cleaning surpasses that because it is an act of kindness that will leave fond memories of you in the minds of your loved ones. They will think of you nicely especially as you did not elongate their grieving process by causing them to go through all that you own. In this way, death cleaning achieves two purposes.

It motivates you to acquire less while leading an organized life and it eases the decision making about your belongings while the people you left behind are grieving. Granted, we will all die without an announcement so there will be something left for your heirs to go through.

These possessions that you will definitely leave behind should be well organized and minimal and therefore leave your heirs smiling. They should not be such as give them months and months of worrying and sorting out.

So, to death clean is to keep your home orderly when you think your years are coming to an end. Magnusson puts this aptly when she said 'a loved one wishes to inherit nice things from you. Not all things from you.'

Death cleaning is also a home organization

strategy and a decluttering concept that helps us keep unnecessary possessions out of the door and keeps our homes looking nice. This makes it something that anyone can practice. It is not a task meant for the elderly alone.

You can begin to death clean irrespective of your age. Look around your house. Chances are you do not need half the things that you have and many of them have been without use for a really long time. The majority of us are hoarders and our generation is a consumer generation. We buy virtually everything we see. Whether or not we need them. We try to follow trends and we just store lots and lots of things that we do not need. In the end, the value we place on these things wane and we no longer even like them. But we hold on to them anyway and end up with houses that look like stores. At every part of our house, we have a large number of material things stored away that we do not use.

Through the concept of death cleaning, the Swedes are telling us to bring those out, decide what to do with them and then do it.

When you think about it, there are lots of people in the same society and community as us that cannot afford any of those things. Also, there are a lot of people around us even within our friends and family that love those things and will appreciate a gift from us.

So, why not organize your home, declutter it by shedding your possessions and end up with a lot of space that not only allows fresh air into your house but also leaves your house looking really nice? Why not try death cleaning?

TIMING OF DEATH CLEANING

We all love to gather possessions and even if you take the love away, accumulating material things is not something we can run away from. In fact, it is the mark of a long life.

That being the case and considering the enormous benefits of death cleaning, how do we know that it is time for us to start decluttering? Death cleaning offers us the opportunity to examine our lives and to celebrate our victories as well as the little joys that make up many years of living. As a result, it ought to be a thoughtful and methodical process during which we can reflect on our lives. This means that it is not something we ought to rush.

In spite of this, decluttering your house while taking your belongings one at a time will take you a long time to achieve. This is why it is better for you to begin early. But how do you know when to start?

The proper time to begin death cleaning has

to do with when you begin to reflect on your mortality knowing that you cannot predict what each day holds. When you begin to think that your time to leave this world is getting closer then you have to start death cleaning.

Some experts predict that this is around the age of sixty-five and above while others say that death cleaning should begin once you are above fifty years of age. Death cleaning could start earlier though if you want to use the concept to make your home tidier.

Thus, the moment your house looks like a mess with the closet door unable to close and no passageway in the store, then you know that you are due for death cleaning. When you use it this way, it will not matter how old you are. Also, if you want to use the Swedish decluttering concept to inculcate self-discipline into yourself or your children, your age will not matter.

The timing of death cleaning is therefore relative to the situation. Elderly people use it to 'set their affairs in order' and by so doing ease the burden of organizing their belongings that they would have dumped on their heirs. But everyone younger can use it to live more organized lives. So, the timing that you choose will depend on your purpose for doing it. If you are one to postpone your death cleaning process however, you will become forced to do it by life itself when you start to age.

You do not want to leave the struggles that come with sorting a beloved deceased person's possessions. Either way, death cleaning ought to start sooner rather than later. This is so true because it is the sort of activity that will take you years to get through. Also, you cannot stop death cleaning once you have started. You have to ensure that you do not slip back to where you began and then end up with a house full of unwanted possessions. This means that death cleaning is a continuous process. One that you cannot stall.

The fact that some people think of dying earlier than others makes the timing of death cleaning different from person to person. Nevertheless, death cleaning must begin as soon as possible rather than as late as we can postpone it. One more thing you should know is that if you do not start death cleaning early, you may never get to do it. It is like developing a habit and it is a healthy habit indeed to develop. In fact, the more time you apportion to death cleaning, the more results you will get and the easier the process will become.

Step by Step Guide to Death Cleaning

Once you have begun your death cleaning, you will realize that it gets easier over time. It gets easier with practice. It can be an onerous task finding a purpose for each of the things we own. This is why death cleaning should be at your pace. Take your time. Slowly. Carefully. While taking time to reflect on each item. If you are a hoarder, you will need to put in some effort into preparing to death clean. You will need to discipline yourself not to acquire more items.

Otherwise, any death cleaning you achieve will be a huge waste of time because you are just going to get out there one day and begin accumulating newer things. So, prepare for death cleaning before you actually start the process. While you are at it, do it at your own pace and devise a means to make it meaningful to you. Death cleaning may take years and once you make it a lifestyle, it would become something you do year in and year out. In fact, the Swedes use dostadning to declutter their houses three times a year.

To enable you succeed at your death cleaning goals, you need to have a method in place. You need to know where to start and where to end so that you do not go about it in a random manner that only ends up leaving your house more disorganized and in turn saps your energy. We have outlined a step by step guide below that you will find helpful.

Where to Start

As you stand in the center of your home looking at all the things you need to deal with, you might become overwhelmed. The first problem you will face is what to begin with. Start your death cleaning by sorting out things you do not want and things you do not use.

As you go from room to room, pull out those

things you no longer use and those that you dislike or do not want and decide what to do with them before you face the rest. It could be things that you think will make your family and friends sad after you are gone or things that will hurt their memory of you. This would include things like letters to your ex, your diary (if it includes anything negative or private) or an odd gift.

Remove all unwanted presents and anything you have in surplus and keep them on their way out of your house. Also, remove anything that may cause your family embarrassment and anything that may reopen painful memories or upset them.

Your Death Cleaning Attitude

When you are death cleaning, you should approach it with a generous mind. Don't hold on emotionally to things that you do not need or that are of no use to you. Also, do not be wasteful.

Think about who may benefit from the things that are left after you have decluttered and give it to them rather than trashing it. Throwing out unwanted things should not be your first step.

Evaluate Each Item

As you go about the process, ask yourself what usefulness each item holds and whether it will be a burden or a blessing to your heirs. Retain only things that will be useful to them. Not things that they will end up throwing away.

For things that your friends and family will love and that you no longer use, give it to them and enjoy watching them use it. Don't hoard it and anticipate that they will pick it once you die. You can even ask each person what they want. Items that are not useful now or in the future should be taken out of your home. Decide what is worth keeping and what should be thrown out by asking yourself if the item will make anyone happier. For items that you want to use or keep until you die and that you have specific wishes regarding what should be done with them after your death, you can leave notes. Attach notes to clothes, books, plates and so on telling your loved ones what you want them to do with each item.

Clothes

The best place to start your death cleaning is in your closet. No matter how many clothes you have, these are more likely to spark off memories that you do not want. This is because even if you have attachments to your clothes, such clothes will not be all over the closet. They will be few.

When you are set to begin your death cleaning therefore, open your closet door and sort through your clothes. Chances are you have so many of them. If you are like most people, a large number of that so many have been unworn for years. Remove all the clothes that you do not wear often. Then place them in a bag and keep the bag aside. Come back often to check if you have unworn clothes piled up again. Bag these and keep aside.

Kitchen

Go through your kitchen cabinet and determine what you currently use each item for. We all keep a little more plates than we need. Remove all items that you do not use as well as those you do not want or that you may dislike. Keep them aside and give them to your loved ones. If you have people visiting you, you can tuck it into their hands as presents. They will appreciate it. A set of plates for example can make great gifts. Do not leave any of your kitchen items untouched. Be sure to check any items that are stored away and forgotten and give them out.

Books

Books are my favorite because we can amass a huge number of them without even knowing. On top of this, they can create a mess when they have not been opened for a long time as they could invite termites to come have a feast when they have been stored and unchecked. Donating or gifting a valuable book is also a very thoughtful thing to do. So go through your book shelves and check for books that you no longer need. It may be that you have read them over and over or you have never read them at all. They are only creating a clutter. If the books are in good condition and you want to make some money from them then sell them as used books.

You can also give them to your friends, children and grandchildren and share knowledge along the way. You might want to hold on to your favorite ones though and you can attach notes in between if you have specific people you want to have them after your death. It is also common for us to have books that are not ours. Return those to the owners or leave instructions regarding that. A book's original place may be at the local library and you should make sure it gets back there and not be an additional mass of clutter in your home.

Pets

If you are the type who keeps lots of pets, then your death cleaning will not be done unless you do something about them. You can choose to donate them or give them out as presents to family members and friends that may love them. However, pets can be good company in your later years when all the kids are gone and your spouse is no longer with you. As a result, you might want to hold on to your pets a little longer. They can give you some comfort and security in the presence of another living thing in your home.

Furniture

Perhaps the most tedious part of death cleaning is deciding what to do with your furniture. This is because if you are elderly, the type of furniture you use, for example mahogany, may no longer be a good fit for your children. They may not like or want them. Also, there may be no market for your furniture. Since they are no longer in vogue, no one will be willing to buy them.

Disposing off your furniture will therefore cost you a little research. You can donate them off to charities who may need them but you need to find out exactly which charities do. Otherwise your furniture will be left to waste away somewhere.

Personal Effects

Your personal effects are the last place for you to visit with your death cleaning exercise. These include letters, photographs and journals. If you start with any of these, you will end up procrastinating the whole exercise because of the emotional outburst that can follow going through old photos or reading old journal logs or love letters.

If you have had a long life however, these items could achieve the opposite and spark joy along the way. Also, some of these items might be of value only to you. They are likely not going to mean anything much to others. Sort these things out and keep them aside in a box. For the photographs, you can declutter them by digitizing them. You can also digitize old videos as well. Your children and grandchildren can help you do this.

Storage

Go through your storage space, attic, basement and garage to check for items that are hidden there and decide what to do with them accordingly. Make sure you check every part of your house for items that will need to be cleaned out or kept for your use.

Remember that what should guide you through your death cleaning exercise is the usefulness of each item at the present moment or sometime in the future. Also, check if there is anyone that the item will be useful to or that the item will bring more joy to. Items that have no use attached to them for you or for anyone else will naturally have to be thrown away.

CHAPTER TWO

ASPECTS OF DEATH CLEANING

We generally like to group things. When you are sorting out all that you own, this will unavoidably extend to things that are not stored up in your house. Death cleaning posits that you leave no stone unturned because your heirs cannot avoid them either.

They would have to face every single thing

that constituted your accumulated possessions. Thus, death cleaning can be grouped. We will concern ourselves with three aspects of death cleaning which are digital death cleaning, physical death cleaning and financial death cleaning. To take stock of and properly manage all these would be to have led an organized life especially during your later years.

Digital Death Management

Our lives are becoming digitized with each passing moment. We are relying on the

Internet more and more for our everyday needs. As a result, we have a lot of accounts on-line. The same goes for social media. I have personally experienced the pain that comes with going through a deceased person's social media account. With people who did not put in place a method to erase all their on-line activity, their family finds it difficult to access any of their digital accounts.

The situation is not usually pretty at all. And of course, you would want your family members to be able to do something about your on-line content once you are gone. If you feel this way, you need to put a system in place to facilitate that. Keep a book of passwords for example where you write all your passwords against the relevant accounts. Merely telling your children your passwords will not take care of the situation because over time the number of passwords you have becomes large. You are likely not going to remember them all and neither will your children.

If you put them down in writing however, your children can easily access any of your social media accounts as well as other accounts you have on-line when you are no longer around. This can make this part of your life more easily managed. Keep the book of passwords somewhere that it will be easy to find.

The issue of digital death management is likely to become increasingly popular and some people have expressed views going to show that in the future people will begin to hire digital death managers to take care of their on-line data.

I cannot express how relieving it feels to see

that the traces of a dead friend on social media have been cleaned out. Digital death managers will be responsible for this. But your own family can become your digital death manager making sure that spontaneous memories of you do not spill out of your on-line content. They would also make sure that all data that may be useful to them is retrieved. You can help them by making all of your on-line content easily accessible.

These content could include music, pictures, letters or even commercial sales pages and royalties. If your family cannot get hold of those then they will just go to waste. We may also have on-line data that we would prefer to deal with ourselves. These could include such things that are capable of hurting the memories we leave behind. Death cleaning your digital content gives you the chance to do that.

Physical Death Management

By physical death management, I mean the aspects of your possessions that you can see around you and touch. These are mostly your material belongings that you have stored up in your house.

Physical death management is the major thrust of death cleaning. It posits that you leave behind minimal possessions that are easy to handle. It also has a lot to do with your living space. That is, the things you hoard in your house. Move around your house with a bag and put on an apron that has a large pocket. Put things you no longer need as you come across them into the bag or the pocket of your apron.

Start with the big items lying around your

house and end with those small in size like photographs. After you have done this, you will need to decide what to do with each item. You will need to decide whether to keep the item or to clean it out.

Death Cleaning Your Money At The Bank

Taking care of a deceased person's bank accounts is one of the most tedious part of managing such deceased estate. Whoever is clearing out the estate has to go from one organization to the other to provide the bank with documents that show that the account holder is dead and that they have the authority to deal with the account. But what is more tedious than this is the administrator of the estate getting to know which financial institutions the deceased person uses. Another evolving trend is using banks that operate wholly on-line. Then there is the issue of the deceased person's credit cards, credit reports and so on. Death cleaning can help you keep this a little more organized before the day comes. You can death clean your money at the bank.

All you need to do is create a document as in the case of your on-line content where you write down your login information for your financial institutions. Write down your passwords and the names of these institutions. Keep the document in a place that it will be easy to find after your death. This way, your administrator will find it easier to access your money in the bank and your heirs in turn will be able to access it.

CHAPTER THREE

WORKING THROUGH THE EMOTIONS INVOLVED WITH DEATH CLEANING

The death cleaning exercise can spark off unwanted emotions. It can also spark off memories and nostalgic feelings. To properly death clean, you will need to work yourself and your family through it.

You will need to deal with negative memories as you find a note, a letter or a diary filled with negative thoughts. If you view death cleaning appropriately though, it should be a revitalizing exercise especially if you have lived a long and fulfilling life.

Communicating Your Intentions To Your Family

It is essential to Swedish death cleaning that you carry others along. Thus, you do not death clean secretly. Tell your friends and family about it and allow as many people that want to be present to come. When you do this, you will be held accountable and be more likely to follow through with your plan. Swedish death cleaning is also a great avenue to let your family know what your final wishes may be. Dostadning involves being able to talk about death without fear. It enables such conversations to take place. Let your family know that you are about to death clean as this can be a way to open up conversations about death.

Most children are afraid to talk about death but you can help them by bringing up death cleaning. Talking about death and dying can make grieving less painful in the future. In the same way, going through a deceased loved one's possessions can make the pain of losing them more acute. So it is good to talk about it and if your children are scared of talking about death then try initiating the conversation with death cleaning.

Make them understand that death is inevitable and that by death cleaning, you are not suggesting that you will be dead soon. Explain to them that it is okay to talk about death. Cheerfully accept whatever help they have to offer as you will find this valuable. There may be items that you cannot move alone for example. They would be of great help moving such items. They might also like some of your things. Maintain a cheerful disposition when you tell them what you are up to. This way, you will not trigger the unwanted dread of death that they likely have already.

Reconnecting With Old Friends

Death cleaning can be a time to catch up with your old friends. Tell all your friends you will be death cleaning. Turn it into a party and invite everyone of them over. Have them go through your things along with your family members to see if there is any they want or that they would like you to donate. Allow them to point out to you the things they want from those items you want to give away. Sit around with them and laugh and reminisce on old times. You can even encourage them to start death cleaning themselves.

If you think that your friends are such as will end up wanting the same things, then give them your possessions as gifts instead. This way, you can choose what you give to who and they will gladly accept it. Try to make them value it by giving each person something that they have always admired. Thus you can reach out to your friends no matter how long ago you have heard from them through your death cleaning exercise.

Decluttering Your Personal Items

It can be overwhelming to have a lot of possessions to deal with. You can figuratively drown in them and when you pick each item, you can have a hard time dealing with it. The answer to whether or not it benefits anyone may therefore be hard to sort out.

At this stage, it can be very beneficial for you to just store them away. Keep items that you are undecided about in a box. You can label it 'undecided' and come back to it when you are done sorting out the things that you are decisive about. We have mentioned elsewhere in this book that giving can be a good way to declutter.

Before you think of throwing your things away, first think about giving them out as presents. They could be books, shoes, clothes and so on. Try to give things that you know the recipient will love. Give thoughtfully. Think about where you are transferring the item to. Does this object fit the taste of the recipient? Do they have space for it in their home? Giving thoughtfully will end up giving you joy because you know that the item is being properly used in its new home. Bring out your box of unwanted clothes and show them to your children. Leave those that nobody wants in the box and label it 'donations'. Give these away to charities and put a smile on someone else's face. Take the box with the photographs and other things that mean something to you alone and label it 'throw away'. Hold on to items that spark off special memories like a vacation with your significant other in your throw away box. Keep your travel collections and odd looking objects like shells or stones that you gathered on trips to different places and that you love in the box as well. With the box properly labelled, even if your family looks through it, it will be with your permission after which they can do away with it.

Handling Stuff You Can't Get Rid Of

After you have sold, donated and given presents, you are likely to have items left that you do not want but are lying around your house. What can you do with these? These may even be items that you cannot get rid of but that are not going to be used by you as you go about your everyday life. Such items include family heirlooms, medals, your children's art projects and other things that fit this description.

Some of these things may not be good for

the trash bin either. They may be things of value but to no one in particular. You can gather these sorts of things together and put them in a box that you label 'important'. While you are still alive, you can enjoy the joys of going through them and when you are dead, your children will know not to throw these away. They would also store them up in their houses and pass it on from one generation to another. Another way to handle these items is to give them away in your will.

CHAPTER FOUR

PREPARING FOR WHAT COMES AFTER

Death cleaning can be emotional but these emotions can be joyful depending on how you approach the exercise. This means that your approach to death cleaning is important. But as you death clean, you must begin to think about the future. You must also begin to prepare for your new life. The one that comes in your later years after the time you declutter your home. This preparation could range from changing where you live to dealing with the emotional side of death cleaning. And this preparation is important to help you enjoy living all the years you have left.

MOVING TO A SMALLER PLACE

At some point, you might want to move to a smaller place. This can be beneficial to you if you are elderly and living alone with no children or grandchildren around. A smaller apartment will make it easier to move around especially with your newly decluttered belongings. But first, you will have to successfully dispose off your house as well. You can leave it to any of your children or you can sell it.

Your children can help you with moving your things or you can seek professional help to do this. There are move managers who can help you to do this. They specialize in helping the elderly downsize their homes to something smaller. If downsizing is not your option, you can also seek help with moving the rest of your property to your new apartment. The homes where your children were raised will undoubtedly be large but you would no longer need houses that large in your later years after the children are all gone.

If you want to sell out your house despite not being elderly, death cleaning can prove beneficial to you as well because having a house with streamlined belongings will boost its value in the eyes of potential buyers who are already seeing it with their things fitted into it.

UNDERSTANDING THAT DEATH CLEANING IS NOT SAD

Death cleaning is not a sad exercise. It should spark joy to go through all that you have acquired over your life. Do not allow feelings of nostalgia to overwhelm and keep you from the purpose of your death cleaning exercise.

It is a considerate way to make sure that your house is not a mess. It is also something that can go on and on for years. As a result, there is no reason to be sad about it. It is a way to gift your kindness to your heirs and a way to live a tidy and more organized life. So you should go through the death cleaning exercise with an open mind and with all the positive outlook that you can muster.

Death cleaning when you are sad or depressed will only achieve adverse results which are not the intention of the Swedish decluttering strategy at all. Therefore, start when you are in a good frame of mind and when you can laugh at all the good things you have in your life. Involve friends and family and turn it into a party and death

cleaning can be one of the nicest things you
have done for yourself.

COMING TO TERMS WITH THE SITUATION

Bring yourself into the death cleaning mode
with a generous mind and a grateful heart.
Death cleaning is a time for you to reflect on
a life well lived. So embrace the situation
and free up whatever is holding you back.
Realize that you are doing this for your own
wellbeing and for the wellbeing of your
loved ones. Realize too that you do not need
to own so much to love living life. In fact,

you can love objects and admire them without owning them. And this should be your new attitude. Think about the disadvantages that a house full of possessions can cause you, such as stress and worry.

Think of death cleaning as a way to release yourself from all of the negativity and make your life tidier, organized and much more enjoyable.

FORGIVING YOURSELF AND EVERYONE ELSE

As I have already pointed out, death cleaning can spark emotions. As you go through the photographs you might well go down memory lane which is why you have to keep them until last. But it is not only photographs that can make you remember the past. A lot of your belongings can do that.

There might be decisions that you have taken that have negatively affected your life and there might be people in your life that you need to forgive. Death cleaning is a good time to do this because it affords us the opportunity to reflect upon our lives. You should consciously let those people and those things go. You should consciously forgive them.

More importantly, forgive yourself for taking decisions that affected the course of your life negatively. Forgive yourself for all the wrongs you might have done. Forgive yourself for holding on to negativity and allow yourself to breathe.

So death cleaning is giving yourself a chance to let go. A chance to forgive you and to forgive everyone else.

CHAPTER FIVE

LETTING GO

So you need to really let go, both in your mind and in your actions. Walk up to old friends who have hurt you and talk about the situation. Then let them know that you have forgiven them.

Another aspect to letting go is taking care of the final details of your life. Something that would make your death cleaning efforts much more worth your while and something we are going to talk about in this chapter.

PREPARING A WILL

Perhaps one of the most important things that you will do to organize your affairs is to prepare your will. This is the most explicit way to make your wishes known. You can write your will yourself or you can engage a solicitor to do so.

Writing a will is a relatively simple process. It depends entirely on the complexity of your property. Thus, if your properties are many and your formula for distributing them is complex, then preparing your will will be a complex process. If they are few, the preparation of your will will also be straightforward. You can get free templates for preparing your will on the Internet that will serve as a guide to help you through the process.

There are a few things you should take into consideration when preparing your will. These include who your executor would be, who your successors would be and the extent of your assets. Your will has to be properly executed. This means that you have to sign it in the presence of two witnesses, who will also sign in the presence of each other.

Thus, you must carefully select your witnesses. If you have children who are under the legal age, you will need to appoint a guardian for them. You must take particular care to include all your properties and all your heirs in your will. Your heirs are called your beneficiaries. You can also state any final wishes that you have in your will. Wills have a format which the templates will guide you through.

The format will include an introduction, a middle and an end. By preparing a will, you proactively prevent any chaos that might happen in the event of your death. You can also cover all members of your family properly and make sure that each person gets something from you. Aside that, you can be sure that they get exactly what you want them to have and in the proportion that you want it to be. Like death cleaning, if you have been thinking of death or if you are beginning to age, you should consider writing a will.

If you want to make the process of distributing your assets easier for your loved ones by preparing your will, then you may find this guide useful:

1. Make a list of your assets

Your assets include your real estate, bank accounts, family heirlooms, vehicles, investments, furniture and other properties. List them out on paper so that you do not leave anything out.

2. Make a list of your beneficiaries

Your beneficiaries are your heirs who you want to give a portion of your assets. Make a list of them so that you do not leave anybody out. Also, write out their legal names, their addresses, their contact information and any other personal details.

3. Include your bequests

Write down against each beneficiary what you want them to get. This will give you clarity for the actual preparation of the will and it will also help you not to forget anything or leave anyone out.

4. Identify your executor(s) $GARRY$

Your executor is the person you are entrusting to make sure that your wishes as outlined in your will are obeyed. He is responsible for administering your estate and making sure your assets are distributed as you have instructed. Choose your executor carefully. He will pay for your funeral costs, settle your debts, your mortgages and your taxes or any taxes accruing from administering your estate.

Make sure that the person you are choosing will be willing to go through that for you. Also, you will need to choose a second executor in case this person fails in performing his duties. Choose people that you can trust.

The requirements for preparing a will are

different from State to State. If you want to prepare your will by yourself, you will need to be acquainted with the statutory requirements in your State. Also, you will need to notarize it to make it legally valid. If you are using the services of a solicitor, the original lists you made will help guide the solicitor through the process.

It is important that your executor knows where the original copy of your will is kept. If your desires change, you can effect the changes in a separate document called a codicil which will also be prepared according to the laws regulating wills in your State. This document must also be witnessed and notarized.

Make sure that you review your will every five years or anytime you experience a major family event like a divorce, a marriage, a birth, a death, an adoption and so on. Your will should include all these changes.

Your will is a crucial part of your death cleaning exercise because it directs your loved ones as to what you want to be done with your assets or who you want to have what. It therefore reduces or totally eradicates any misunderstanding they would have had.

LEAVING DIRECTIVES BEHIND

You can leave directives for your loved ones through your will, through notes attached to your possessions and through documents that you have kept where they could easily find them. You can even leave instructions regarding your burial wishes.

You can leave directives concerning what you want to be done with family heirlooms. This is a valid way to remain in the minds of your loved ones. Death cleaning encourages that you leave directions as to what you want your survivors to do with the things you could not give away during your life because that way you save them a lot of pain, confusion and tears. This is the best gift you can give to them. The pain that comes with the death of a loved one should not be further aggravated.

LIVING THE REST OF YOUR LIFE IN BLISS AND PEACE

It is clear to you by now that Swedish death

cleaning is a process. It is not a once and for all thing. You have to stay on track and ensure that you are not accumulating newer items as this would take you back to the beginning of your death cleaning exercise. Also, the time invested will become wasted.

Death cleaning is hard but not sad. It is hard because of the enormous work to do and the time that it would take. It is also hard because of the possibility of revisiting the past during the exercise.

Once you are done with it, you'll have to move on with enjoying your life. The first step to living the rest of your life in bliss and peace is to reward yourself for a job well done. There are a whole lot of things you can do which include taking walks, getting a massage, taking yourself out to lunch or dinner, baking, spending time with your friends and so on. This way, your attention is shifted to the present. You must do all you can to enjoy peace and happiness for the rest of your life. Go out more.

Meet your new neighbors and laugh. Watch out for accumulation though. Don't reward yourself by buying lots of new items. Learn how to love an item and appreciate it without ending up with it in your shopping bag.

Keep your home decluttered by checking from time to time to see if there are items that you do not use. Keep such items stored away or given out. Some people suggest that you store such items away in a box that you keep underneath your bed. Swedish death cleaning helps you to develop useful habits that you can use from now onwards. Be cautious about the things you accumulate and let your new habits guide you to living a more organized life.

CONCLUSION

It would appear that the Swedish decluttering concept 'death cleaning' aims at redirecting our lives unto the things that are most important in life. It is more important to put smiles on faces and see those smiles than it is to acquire more possessions than everyone else. It is more honorable to give all you have away to people who need them than it is to die with a lot of them. When you give, you will enjoy a decluttered home. One that does not have unused possessions stacked up at every corner. These two are obviously some of the biggest benefits of Swedish death cleaning.

So Why Is Death Cleaning So Important Anyway?

I stated earlier that death cleaning is medically known to reduce stress. I have also pointed out that it is an avenue to give to others and to enjoy a decluttered home in return. Here are some of the biggest benefits of death cleaning that may get you to act on it right away.

1. Communication

Death cleaning opens the lines of communication between elderly parents and their children about death. If death is lurking by the corner, it would as well be beneficial to everyone to get the family to talk about it. This will reduce the shock when it actually happens. It will also help the survivors to gain greater balance over the situation. By death cleaning, you can also communicate your final wishes to members of your family if you have any.

2. You can walk around your house a little bit more

By death cleaning, you are able to free up space in your home which not only makes it look nicer but also makes it more comfortable and enjoyable.

3. Happiness

Getting to see your loved ones actually use your things while you are still alive will result in a lot of happiness for you. In the same way, being able to give also brings the sort of joy that you will experience as you make donations to charities and other people that love and need your items. It will redirect your priorities to people as the most important thing in life.

4. Stress Reduction

Death cleaning can elongate your life because studies have shown that a house full of clutter can increase stress, increase anxiety and render you unproductive. If you are like most people, then you are always anxious when your home is unorganized and full of things that you probably do not even need. Thinking about what to do with them is enough to cause you stress and death cleaning is a way to deal with that.

5. Organization

When your house is full of stuff, you will be more likely to lose things that are important to you like receipts and bills. Death cleaning keeps your house organized and you will easily locate items that you want to use. When you death clean, you will no longer need to spend hours looking for particular items.

6. Safety

A decluttered house makes it easier to move

around and reduces the risk of domestic accidents.

7. Reduces Estate Management Disputes

Death cleaning can help you keep your loved ones from fighting over your estate. This is because you have put in place a system that makes everything easy to manage and you have also left directives behind.

8. Reduces Grief

Death cleaning is your own way of reducing your loved ones' grief after your death. The more time they spend going through your possessions, the more pain they will experience. You can reduce this pain by death cleaning.

9. Tax exemptions

When you make donations and itemize them, you will be able to use the list to get a tax break.

10. Gifting Family History to the Next Generation

By death cleaning, you can pass on to your children and grandchildren objects that have being in the family and means a lot to the family. You can also walk them through stories peculiar to your family and each object can inspire a family reunion when you get to talk about them.

So death cleaning is gifting peace and a tidy life to yourself and gifting kindness to your loved ones.

What If You Are An Elderly Person's Child Reading This Book?

In some situations, elderly parents might be

the ones who are not open to the idea of death cleaning. You may be wanting to initiate the death cleaning conversation with your parents. You are going to be doing this at the risk of looking like you have been thinking about their death. So, what is the appropriate way to go about it?

You do not convince your parents to death clean by just walking up to them and telling them that you want to help them organize their things before they die. They will be uninterested in your suggestion and will just end up worrying. You have to be considerate and kind. You have to keep at the back of your mind that talking through their belongings will help you know their wishes for each item rather than guessing which items mattered to them and what they would have wanted you to do with what. So, you are doing this for you as much as for them.

The best way to begin the death cleaning conversation with a parent is to emphasize the benefits. For example, ask them if they would love to have help with organizing their belongings so that their house is more enjoyable to live in. Do not give up on the idea if your parent is not receptive.

You will need to have the conversation over and over to get such parent to consider your idea. Another way to get your parents to death clean is to open up discussions about the objects in their house.

When you walk through history with them, they will be more likely to listen to anything you have to say.

My Death Cleaning Experience

Before my grandmother exited the world,

she usually loved having us around and each time we visited, she had something ready to give to us as some sort of thank you present. They were usually lovely and many weren't but we accepted them anyway.

She always gave these away with a sense of joy that I could see in her face. When the day finally came, she had few possessions that we could hassle over. It was like she had been preparing for this. Then I had no idea what she was doing but now it is quite clear to me that that was her idea of death cleaning. The china plates, the table clothes and other odd gifts were her way of death cleaning and one that decluttered her home afterwards. Now that the Swedes have reminded us of the wisdom in their culture, I am set to begin my own death cleaning.

FINAL THOUGHTS ON DEATH CLEANING

Swedish Death cleaning is a thoughtful way to redirect our lives from the objects that we accumulate to the people in our lives; to the memories we have created and to life itself. It is a way to give more meaning to our lives and recognize that our possessions do not define us. Rather, what defines us is our kindness towards others. Also, it reminds us that to live a meaningful life is to reach out with love to other people and to create great adventures that will in turn become great memories.

Swedish death cleaning also offers us an opportunity to reflect on the past. It offers us the opportunity to laugh at the adventure that is our life and the opportunity to reconnect with the people in our present.

1ST

Clothes Remove Those you
        do not wear

2nd Kitchen cupboards
    Remove Those you do
not use, OR do not want or
dislike give away or give
to charity shops or give as
gifts to friends or family

Books — same —

Furniture —
      Later

Personel Efects /
Photo's ⎱— Last — Jewelry
Keepsakes (family)
Pictures

Will — Done ✓

Printed in Germany
by Amazon Distribution
GmbH, Leipzig